AF28 72

Hans-Georg Renner & Melanie Rupp

Why the lime tree

has heart-shaped leaves

A love fairy tale

Imprint

Bibliographic information of the German National Library:

The German National Library lists this publication in the German National Bibliography; detailed bibliographic data are available on the Internet at http://dnb.dnb.de.

© 2023 Hans-Georg Renner / Melanie Rupp

Production and publishing house: BoD – Books on Demand, Norderstedt, Germany

ISBN: 978-3-7583-0196-4

Why the lime tree

has heart-shaped leaves

Once upon a time ...

a long, long time ago in a small village

... perhaps very close to you ...

In this village, it happened that on the day of the beginning of spring, three children were born.

Sofia, Elwin and Finn.

The three children got along splendidly and the two boys, Elwin and Finn, became closest friends.

The children grew and matured

and Elwin took over more and more of his parents'
tailoring.

Finn now ran his parents' forge and gaffs,

the two-pointed forks, were his speciality.

Sofia had become a good businesswoman

and ran her parents' business.

PILS
RECHNUNGEN

When the three were young adults,

both Elwin and Finn

testified their love for Sofia.

Sofia loved them both very much,

but she couldn't quite decide between

the two young men.

As a result, Elwin and Finn's friendship suffered and there were more and more disagreements between them.

At first, this was smiled at in the small village.

But more and more, Elwin's and Finn's families were becoming divided.

The atmosphere in the village deteriorated and the small village threatened to fall into two camps.

There were those who wanted to see Elwin and Sofia married and those who would have liked to see Finn and Sofia as a couple.

In order to prevent a threatening split of the small village, the village elder asked Sofia to please decide to whom she would give her word if she wanted to marry.

Since Sofia could not make a deciding with her mind, she made the following decision.

She would let her heart decide and to the man who touched her heart the most with a gift the next morning, she would give her word.

Finn was sad. He was poor and did not know what to give Sofia. Saddened, he walked through the village and passed the village lime tree.

He loved this tree and had often retreated to it when something was troubling him.

So, Finn climbed into the lime tree and sat down on a thick branch.

He thought of Sofia all the time, took his scissors from his tool belt and cut a heart out of a lime leaf, and another and another, all night long.

At dawn, Finn climbed wearily down from the lime tree and fell asleep right on the trunk.

But this was the morning when Sofia was expecting Elwin and Finn ...

Elwin came to Sofia and proudly presented her with his coins in a minstrel's box.

The box was carved from the finest wood.

According to an old custom, the man brought the first gift to his chosen one in it and Sofia was delighted.

Now she waited for Finn, but he did not come ...

But Sofia also wanted to give Finn the opportunity to woo her, so she went to find him.

On her way, she passed the village lime tree.

She stopped, deeply moved. For Finn was sitting under a tree full of leaves in the shape of a heart.

Tears of joy welled up in her eyes...

and her heart began to melt and throb loudly at the same time.

Sofia ran to Finn and hugged him overjoyed. She had seen how great his love for her was and was deeply touched by his gift.

Under the linden tree she promised to marry him.

Nature was so moved by this love that since that time every lime tree in the world has had heart-shaped leaves.

End

"Why the lime tree has heart-shaped leaves" *

Retold by Hans-Georg Renner

Illustrated by Melanie Rupp

Contact: hello@love-around-the-world.com

* Unfortunately, the source of this love fairy tale is unknown to us.
We would be pleased to receive any information. Many thanks.

The love fairy tale is available in bookshops, or directly from the BoD publishing house, also in German

"Warum die Linde herzförmige Blätter hat"

ISBN 978-3-7578-3058-8

Appendix

Home for Love

In the US alone, there are over 35,000 museums on a wide variety of topics, but no place for the history and diversity of love.

It's time for a real love museum, a "museum for the cultural history of love".

Contents include love for oneself, positive sexuality, loving relationships between people, families, friends, peoples, to animals, to nature and to our home, the earth.

Our concept also includes interactive elements on stories and "cultures of love".

Impulses of love, friendship and peace will emancte from this place for love, and it will be an asset for us humans, for art, culture and nature.

We are happy if YOU support us.

We want our children and grandchildren to still be able to fall in love with healthy nature, for example under a lime tree.

We ask you to support an environmental protection organisation such as Greenpeace, WWF, or Robin Wood.

If 10% of Americans became members, they would have such political weight that we could stop many climate destructions in our capital-dictatorship.

One idea would be, for example, to give membership as a gift for birthdays.
(Thanks to Anny Hartmann for the tip, in her programme "Klima-Ballerina")

The earth is beautiful